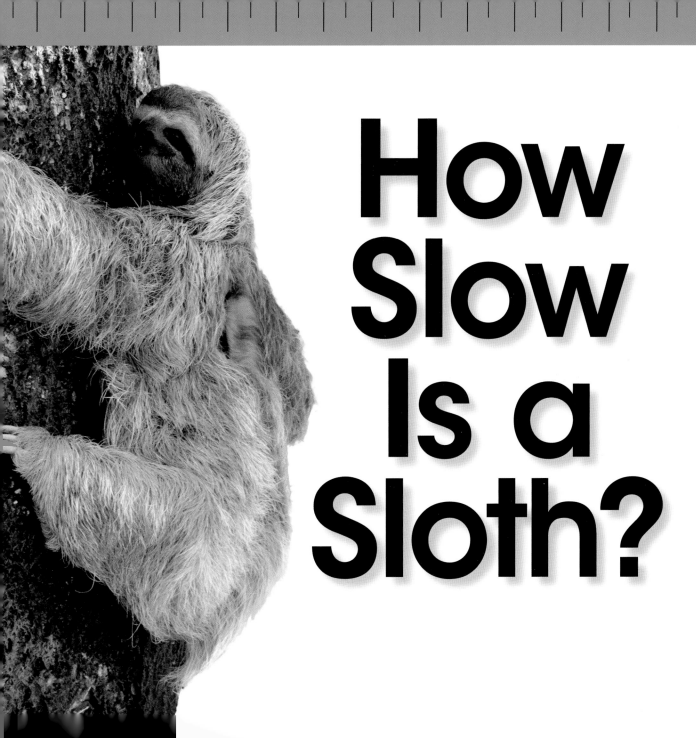

How
Slow
Is a
Sloth?

The Child's World®
childsworld.com

Published by The Child's World®
1980 Lookout Drive • Mankato, MN 56003-1705
800-599-READ • www.childsworld.com

Photographs ©: Keith Hinman/iStockphoto, cover, 1;
Shutterstock Images, 2–3, 4–5, 6, 14, 14–15, 16–17, 20–21; David
Parsons/iStockphoto, 6–7; George Dolgikh/Shutterstock
Images, 8–9; Nacho Such/Shutterstock Images, 10, 23;
Mmphotographie.de/Shutterstock Images, 10–11; Jonathan
C. Photography/Shutterstock Images, 12–13; Martijn Smeets/
Shutterstock Images, 18–19

ISBN 9781503816794
LCCN 2016945834

Printed in the United States of America
PA02325

ABOUT THE AUTHOR

Kurt Waldendorf is a writer and editor.
He lives in Vermont with his wife and their
Old English sheepdog, Charlie.

NOTE FOR PARENTS AND TEACHERS

The Child's World® helps early readers develop their informational-reading skills by providing easy-to-read books that fascinate them and hold their interest. Encourage new readers by following these simple ideas:

BEFORE READING

- Page briefly through the book. Discuss the photos. What does the reader think he or she will learn in this book? Let the child ask questions.
- Look at the glossary together. Discuss the words.

READ THE BOOK

- Now read the book together, or let the child read the book independently.

AFTER READING

- Urge the child to think more. Ask questions such as, "What things are different among the animals shown in this book?"

Sloths are the slowest **mammals** on Earth. How slow is a sloth?

A giant **tortoise** is slow.

But it could beat a sloth in a race.

Sloths move slowly. This saves **energy**. A sloth takes six seconds to crawl the length of a pencil.

Sometimes sloths move faster.

At top speed, a sloth moves the length of a car in one minute.

An adult human
could walk back and
forth across a room
10 times before a sloth
could crawl across
it once.

A cheetah runs quickly. A sloth would take seven minutes to go as far as a cheetah goes in one second.

Sloths climb and live in trees. But it takes a sloth one minute to climb the height of a door.

Even sloth stomachs are slow. It takes a sloth one month to **digest** a meal of leaves.

A sloth moves faster in water. But it would still take a sloth eight minutes to swim across a pool.

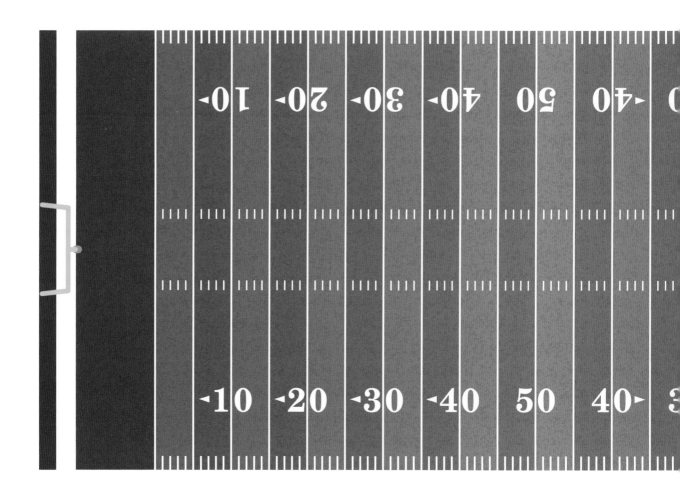

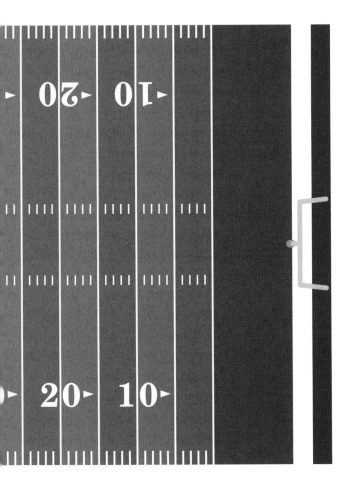

A sloth can only move so far in one day. A sloth would take two days to move across a football field. That is slow!

▶ Sloths live in trees in the rain forest. They have long claws they use to hang from tree branches.

▶ Sloths spend most of their time upside-down. They even sleep upside-down.

▶ Sloths can turn their heads almost all the way around.

▶ Sloths move so slowly that algae grows on their fur. The green color matches the leaves of trees. It makes the sloth harder for other animals to see.

▶ Sloths climb to the ground to go to the bathroom. They only do this about one time per week.

GLOSSARY

digest (di-JEST) To digest is to break down food in the body. A sloth takes a long time to digest its food.

energy (EN-ur-jee) Energy is the ability or strength to do things. A sloth saves energy by moving slowly.

mammals (MAM-uhlz) Mammals are animals with hair or fur. Mammals give birth to live babies.

tortoise (TOR-tuhs) A tortoise is a turtle that lives on land. The giant tortoise is the slowest reptile.

TO LEARN MORE

BOOKS

Loy, Jessica. *Weird & Wild Animal Facts*.
New York, NY: Henry Holt, 2015.

Schuh, Mari C. *Sloths*. Minneapolis, MN: Bullfrog, 2015.

Shuetz, Kari. *Baby Sloths*. Minneapolis, MN: Bellwether, 2014.

WEB SITES

Visit our Web site for links about sloths:
childsworld.com/links

Note to Parents, Teachers, and Librarians: We routinely verify our Web links to make sure they are safe and active sites. So encourage your readers to check them out!

INDEX